DIVINE REVELATION

OPEN LETTER TO THE EARTHMEN

Iyke Nathan Uzorma

DIVINE REVELATION

ISBN: 979-8-89030-044-7 Paperback)
ISBN: 979-8-89030-045-4 (Ebook)

This book was published and printed in the United States of America by Dr. Moses Ayuketa of Christ Restoration Center, through Authorunit.

CHRIST RESTORATION CENTER

CONTACTS:

Authorunit
17130 Van Buren Blvd, Ste 238, Riverside, CA 92504
+1, 877-826-5888
www.authorunitcom

Dr. Moses Ayuketa,
1766 E. 61st Street, Tulsa, Ok 74136
+1, 9188498130
ayuketamoses@gmail.com

Archbishop (Prof.) Iyke Nathan U.,
P. O. Box 1562, Effurun, Warri, Nigeria;
Phone +234-807-563-7746, WhatsApp +234-818-379-6658;
Email: harbingeroffice@gmail.com; www.iykenathanuzorma.org

Contents

Dedication

This treatise is most respectfully dedicated to
THE GREAT LORD JESUS THE CHRIST
For Laying The Foundation Of Light
In The World Of Man

Clarification of Identity

For clarification regarding several inquiries on identity, especially to those who attribute the actions of my younger brother, Prof. Protus Nathan Uzorma, to me, be informed that we are different persons but from same parents. Readers should take note.

-- The author.

Archbishop (Prof) Iyke Nathan Uzorma
HARBINGER OF THE LAST COVENANT

Comments:

"It is indeed a miracle that Prof. Iyke Nathan Uzorma, a well known Guru and Perfect Master of Esoteric Mysteries has been humbled and convicted by the Holy Spirit to acknowledge and accept the sovereignty of the true Christ over his life."

-PROF. OLADEJO OKEDIJI
Former Dean, Faculty of Social Sciences; University of Lagos, Nigeria.

*****

"Though several publications on religious and spiritual matters exist, but from my personal experience, none the world over is as authoritative as the works of Prof. Iyke Nathan Uzorma, Harbinger of the Last Covenant."

-HIS EXCELLENCY,
YURI KWAKU BAAWINE
Former Ambassador of Ghana to Saudi Arabia.

*****

"My meeting Prof. Iyke Nathan Uzorma, Harbinger of the Last Covenant, in Nigeria, greatly lifted my spirit and opened my eyes more on a deeper aspect of the mysteries of life."

-PROF. YOSIAH MAGEMBE BWATWA
Dean, Faculty of Education,
Tumaini University, Dar-es-Salaam, Tanzania.

"We thank God for using in our day and age His Harbinger, Prof. Iyke, to open the eyes of many in his spiritual mission that is divinely bound to move the world",

-CHIEF DONALD UGBAJA, NPM, mni
Deputy Inspector General of Police (rtd.), Abuja, Nigeria

"The Harbinger of the Last Covenant, who was former Occult Grand Master, appears plain and ordinary but, as revealed to me, he is a head lion in the pride of God's lions."

- SUPREME PROPHETESS NNEKA A. Udi-KEN
Founder, Tabitha (Mercy) Prayer Ministry, Effurun, Warri, Nigeria.

"My respected mentor, Prof. Iyke Nathan Uzorma, Harbinger of the Last Covenant, thanks for teaching me the reality of the forces of darkness, their manipulations and weaknesses. Thank you sir and

MayGod continue to use you to bless our generation."

- MOSES AYUKETA
Presiding Bishop, House of Prayer, Christ Restoration Centre, Tulsa, Ok., USA.

"We thank the Almighty God for giving us His

'Harbinger of the Last Covenant', to open our eyes and bring true spiritual awakening in our time"

-HIS ROYAL MAJESTY
- PROF. AMUZIEWA DELE ODIGBO,
Ezeigwe 43rd of Nkwesi kingdom Oguta, Imo State, Nigeria.

*****

"The books of Prof. Iyke Uzorma, Harbinger of the Last Covenant, are nobel and highly enriching to humanity."

- PROF. SMART O. NWAOKORO
Head, Dept. Of Animal Science,
University of Benin, Nigeria.

*****

His Grace, Archbishop

(Prof.) Iyke Nathan Uzorma, Harbinger of the Last Covenant, is a great Messenger of Light that to me his kind has never existed before. There is nothing that the Lord said through him that hasn't come to pass. This includes prophesies to nations, tribes and persons. He has encountered the Lord face to face on numerous occasions. He has encountered the Angels, Archangels, Great Ones of Divine

Light above and Watchers. I think he stands on a higher platform to bring to our world the hidden mysteries that have not been told of old. It is my sincere plea to everyone living on the surface of the world to listen to him. Let the world hear and accept the deep spiritual expositions giving to us by the Lord Himself and His Great ones of Divine Light Above, through the Harbinger of the Last Covenant.

- Oduro Amoh-Yaw Michael
Central Coordinator, The Committee of Light, Ghana

*****

"When great Souls speak, mysteries are demystified, but when the Harbinger of the Last Covenant speaks, great Souls learn wisdom to teach others".

- PASTOR GABRIEL S. OBICHUKWU
Redeemed Christian Church of God, Abakaliki, Nigeria.

*****

DIVINE DECREE

*L*ET THE HEAVEN OF THE HEAVENS BLESS THOSE WHO BLESS THE GOD OF HEAVEN. AMEN. LET THE HEAVEN AND THE EARTH GIVE BIRTH TO THE SPIRIT OF BLESSINGS IN ALL THE FAMILIES OF THE FAITHFUL. AMEN. LET THE SPIRIT OF LIGHT OF JEHOVAH GOD AND HIS CHRIST REIGN SUPREMELY IN ALL THE AFFAIRS OF MEN. AMEN. LET THE WICKEDNESS OF DARKNESS, THE HOSTS THEREOF, BE BURIED IN THE WOMB OF BLOOD. AMEN. LET THE FORCES OF DARKNESS NOT ESCAPE. AMEN.

LET THE FAITHFUL IN THE LIGHT OF THE ALMIGHTY, STANDING THIS DAY UPON THE BOUNDARY OF THE OLD AND NEW, EXCEL IN THE PRIMORDIAL BLESSINGS OF FATHER ABRAHAM, IN THE SPIRIT OF THE RIGHTEOUSNESS OF CHRIST. AMEN. AND LET ALL THOSE WHO WILL FAITHFULLY READ THIS DIVINE REVELATION, WHO ARE COUNTED IN ALL THE FACE OF THE EARTH, RISE IN LIGHT, IN THE POSSESSION OF SPIRITUAL AND MATERIAL FAVOUR, IN THE BENEVOLENCE OF JEHOVAH GOD AND HIS CHRIST, NOW AND FOREVER. AMEN. AMEN. AMEN.

— Harbinger of the Last Covenant.

OPEN LETTER TO THE EARTHMEN
DIVINE REVELATION FOR THE WORLD OF MAN,
BEFORE AND BEYOND 2020 – 2075,
FROM THE GREAT LORD OF THE UNIVERSE
AND MIGHTY ANGELIC ONES ABOVE, THROUGH
THE HARBINGER OF THE LAST COVENANT

Grace be multiplied to you brethren, partners, friends, fans, the faithful, the faithless, lovely and loved ones, foes, readers and the entire children of men. I wish you all Peace from the Glorious Throne of the Almighty Father that abides within you and within which you abide, in the Name of Our Lord Jesus Christ. Amen.

INTRODUCTION

Earthmen, as you may be aware, the world of man is presently encapsulated in a high profile network of darkness and wickedness. No nation on Earth is left out. But in the midst of these, the Supreme Light of the Almighty is also ignited to salvage the children of men, by the Finger of the King of Kings and Lord of Lords.

To this end, you have a duty, I have a duty, we have a duty. What is this duty? It is to always serve as divine channels of the Light of God, for the subjugation of darkness in our world. And what is this Light? It is Love, Divine Love. Let this be manifested in our thoughts, words and actions.

By this, we work and walk within the foundation of the system which grants the entry for the intervention of the Forces of Light in our world; which dovetail our consciousness with THAT ordained to salvage the human race. This is the hour to truly be our brothers keeper. This is the hour of fulfilment, for anyone who is truly human to be a defender of Light.

Let the reader of this material be guided by the Spirit of Light in God, to be properly situated on the systems of the Holy Spirit, for personal and collective excellence in divine ascent. Amen.

A CHAMBER OF LIGHT

Earthmen, you may be aware that the physical realms of Earth are mere reflections of the activities of forces operating beyond the physical systems of reality. The evidence of this abound in diverse forms in our world. And concerning a particular spiritual experience that I had in a certain chamber of the Heavenly realms of Light, beyond the world of man, before the year 2020, even unto the years ahead, regarding our world, let me share but a few here.

In the Spirit, in the realms beyond the world of man, I stood upon a divine chamber. I was lifted up into the realm where the Light of the One Eternal God dominates; the chamber wherein Light alone reigns.

This was in the early hours of the first day of January, 2017. A Great One came to the chamber and stood before me. This was a Watcher, a holy One of Heaven, clothed in a purple robe.

Above was a Throne fading away from the clouds of great Light. And One sat therein – Lord of the Universe, the Lord of Light, Lord of Hosts! He came forth as One of the Supreme Manifestations of the LORD, whose Manifestations are unlimited in eternity. By His command, the Watcher spoke to the Harbinger of the Last Covenant. And of the things said, the things revealed, here are some.

There are specific and special number of humans now on Earth, scattered around different nations, religions, tribes, churches, amongst others, whose roots and subtle blood-origins were traced. These were found in the primordial blood of the righteous, even the blood of the great one, seed of the Abraham – father of mankind. This great one was slain by a vicious mind from 'Nachash' – Prince of Darkness, yet set apart for the increase of the seed of righteousness.

Upon his blood came the magnification of the Holy Blood of the Great Lord Jesus the Christ, shed to salvage the world. And it came to pass in the Heavenly realms of Light that they became one fold under One Shepherd. I observed that a Divine decree was made by the One on the Throne, with His eternal Seal upon it. It was made for some chosen ones on Earth. And to such chosen ones, it was decreed thus:

> ***"Whatever has troubled your life, to hold you down; whatever that is not planted by Me, but has followed you, which finger you witnessed even in the years before now, will not follow you into the years ahead"***.

One came forth in the Spirit -- messenger of falsehood. He had a name resembling the name of 'The One that saved the world by His Blood'. But in his heart lay the manipulations of falsehood, by which he became the Spirit that blocks the ways of others through lies. He was chained and taken away.

Then it was said that all the chosen ones suffering from lies placed on them, in any enclave, stand freed. The garment of lies upon them is removed; the joys of testimony have returned to them. It was clearly shown to me in the higher realms of the Spirit of Light that:

1. The 'hunters', hunters of the precious life, with the attire of harlots, are of increase from the year 2017 to the years ahead, in all the nations of the Earth-world. Guided by the 'mother of iniquity', they will be strengthened in the vicious mission that leads to perdition.
In Nigeria, Ghana, Syria, USA, Malaysia, UK, Brazil, Japan, amongst other places, they will work hard to dominate and ruin those that lead others.

2. When a crime is committed by someone in Italy, the spirit that brought about the crime could be residing in someone in India. This is part of the unknown mysteries of being.

A Chamber of Light A Great Spirit of Light from the Lord Himself has gone forth to search out such, from family to family, in the entire world of man. This began from the year 2017 to the years ahead. Thus, in connection with this, it was said that 'many will die in the world of man, for many to live', as spirits are changed in humans, through interchange, and spirits are returned to primordial origins.

3. In Ogun, Anambra, Sokoto, Niger and Edo States of Nigeria, great trees were given new houses.

4. The spirit of the Beast, in agreement with the heads thereof, will bring forth a system in which the children of men, not the chosen ones, will reap the fruits of death.

5. The table is turned, for the world of man. Power is taken away from the Beast and restored to the chosen ones. The black is made white; the white is made black.
(See: 'Verses of Eternal Truth', by Iyke Nathan Uzorma).

6. Blood, blood, blood: so much blood shed on Earth, filling up the subtle spheres of our world. A mighty cleansing of this, by the Finger of the King of Kings and Lord of Lords, is in motion. Gathered in three spots, it is required unto three great lands.

7. Many will be transferred to long journeys in the sleep state as never before, from the year 2017 to the years ahead, for the change of spirits.

8. On the 10th of May, 2017, great battle fought in the Space, in the realms between

Mars and Earth, between the Forces of Light and the forces of darkness, in which the victory of Light over darkness was enacted, will prolong the lives of the earthmen.

9. For the release of great Souls coming to the physical realms of Earth from the year 2017, many births will occur henceforth in the world of man; even the barren will rejoice.

Now, for the things said but not presented here, I urge you to only hope in the Light of Jehovah God and His Christ, not in the works of man. Be prayerful and seek always to be guided by the Holy Spirit.

THE SEEKER OF BLESSINGS

Now, it happened in the world of man, that an earthman, a faithful one, rose to seek the Holy Face of the Almighty; to seek greater blessings from the Most Merciful, in his home.

By Divine Mercy, the earthman was brought before the Lord, who came forth and manifested as 'The Son of Man'. In the Holy Presence of the Lord of the Universe, he laid low in humility. (This is the path that we must follow in the journey of life, for divine excellence in Light). Therein, like father Abraham of old (Gen. 18:1,2) and the Great Lord Jesus the Christ in the garden of Gethsemane (Math. 26:36-39), the earthman fell on his face and paid his most respectful obeisance to the Supreme Lord, who is the Holiest of the holies. Again, this is the path we must follow.

Then the earthman said to the Lord: **"Oh my Lord, I seek great blessings from Thee, for my survival, for my home, in the world of man".** And the One Eternal Lord, who is Powerful than fire, said to him: **"Peace be with you, son of man. Behold, if you will receive great blessings from Me, return to your abode and carry your cross".**

And it came to pass that the earthman returned to his house. At first he didn't know what his cross was. Throughout the night, he thought over this to no avail. When the morning came, by the leading of his consciousness, through the recognition of his mind rudiments, the earthman reached a definite conclusion.

Consequently, as his wife dressed up for work, he came out, carried her up and placed her on his head. People saw him and were bamboozled. They said to him: **"Oh man, why are you carrying your wife upon your head?"** He answered and said unto them: "The Lord said that I should carry my cross in order to receive His great blessings. My wife is the main cross of my life; that's why I am carrying her thus". **Those who have ears to hear, let them hear.** Earthman, it is said that marriage should be enjoyed not endured. When you enjoy your marriage in love, it won't be a cross of pain to you. And even when you still consider it a cross, it will be a sweet cross. I hear you say that your wife is a cross. I tell you, when you endure your marriage in pain, it becomes a bitter cross to you. Earthman, to the extent that you consider your wife to be the cross of your life, to that extent you are also the cross of her life. If you think that your wife is a bitter cross to you, oh earthman, then of a truth, you are the bitter cross she is carrying right now.

Children of men, let not your life become a cross of pain, a burden, to your fellow human in whatever form. Twice blessed is the man who conducts himself in such a manner that does not bring pain to others, in such a manner that burdens no one in the journey of life. Sevenfold blessed is the one whose words bring peace to the hearts of men, not pain and the rudiments of anger.

When the Lord tells the earthman to go home and carry his cross, with regards to his wife, for the manifestations of greater blessings, what does that mean? Simply stated: it means that you should at all times shower her with love. It means that man should at all times abide by the admonition of one of the ancient sacred writings of Tibet, thus:

"O cherish her, as a blessing sent thee from heaven; let the kindness of thy behaviour endear thee to her heart".

Again, when the Almighty Lord speaks in like manner to the daughter of man, that she should carry her cross, with regards to her husband, what does it entail? The same Tibetan ancient treatise answers thus:

"Submission and obedience are the lessons of her life, and peace and happiness are her reward".

Therefore, Oh children of men, love your wives that greater blessings from above will descend upon you, upon your home, from the Almighty; respect and obey your husbands that happiness and peace will fill your hearts, fill your home. A word is enough for the wise.

DIVINE VISITATION OF THE GREAT LORD JESUS THE CHRIST

During a Christian conference I held in Accra, on the first day of my arrival, I tried to sleep at the night after prayer session but couldn't. Then I spent the night working on my treatise to be published. Exactly by 4.20 am, while my door and windows in the hotel suite remained closed, a wind began to blow in the bedroom.

I got up and went to the parlor, the wind was there, even to the bathroom. It was both strange and glorious. I knelt down, bowed my head to the Almighty Lord and began to pray. As I was praying, a voice said to me: "Son of man, arise". I arose and, behold, the room became something else. Immediately, the environment that I found myself became larger than a football field.

On my right side, I saw what looked like cloud mingling with water and descending from above. Upon this sat the Great Lord Jesus the Christ, who shed His Blood to save the world. By my left side, in front and behind me, were Mighty Hosts of the Forces of Light – great Angelic Beings.

Now, it came to pass that the Lord Himself directed me to raise a song for the welcoming of Himself and the Hosts, and for the guidance and blessings of the children of men. Then the Spirit of the Lord put a glorious song in my heart and I began to sing. I sang for several hours in the Presence of the Lord, whilst the entire experience of the divine visitation, within the framework of time of the earthman, was less than an hour.

As I was singing, joined by the Hosts of Heaven, the Lord became multifarious in a manner that can't be explained; for He entered into each of the Hosts, and it came to pass that He entered into me. Then I became something else, whilst completely retaining the identity of my being. Then He said to me:

> ***"Harbinger of the Last Covenant, raise this song in the midst of those who believe in Me. It is a broom in My Hand to sweep off things that are not planted by Me. Behold, in any gathering, in any enclave, in any home wherein it is raised, wherein I am praised with the purity of heart, unpleasant situations must flee. This is given to you this day; use it at all times, and no matter how difficult a situation is upon anyone that comes to you, in My Name, it must disappear; it must fade away...."***

Then I saw huge sums of money, with silver and gold, that no man can count, rising from the ground to the sky. And a holy one said to me: **"Take these to help the children of men in your world"** . Again I looked and saw a huge flag and another holy one said to me: **"This is the flag (symbol) of divine Mercy of the Lord".** And it was said that I should choose between the manifested wealth and the flag for the people of our world. And I said: **"I choose the divine flag of the Mercy of the Almighty Lord"** . At last, the Lord Himself said to me:

> *"Harbinger of the Last Covenant, go forthwith that which you have chosen; for in My Mercy also lies the wealth shown to you, but in the wealth lies not My Mercy. Let all that seek Me uphold mercy, for this is the hour of great blessings to the faithful in your world".*

After other things He said, He finally ascended with the Hosts, whilst my suite became normal again. In the evening of that day, the glorious song was raised and recorded in the congregation of the faithful; mercy was proclaimed and all were blessed who came with pure hearts. In subsequent occasions, more songs were given to the one saying these things, for the increase of Power and the Blessings to the faithful ones on Earth.

The same Divine Mercy, by the Spirit of the Lord, I proclaim upon you, the reader of this material. May the Mercy of the Almighty Lord radiate more and more in your life; in the entire world of man, in the Holy Name of Christ Our Lord. Amen.

Mercy is all that we need from the Lord of the Universe; without it we won't make progress on the path of Light. **"Blessed are the merciful: for they shall obtain mercy"** (Math. 5:7).

CONTROLLER OF MANIFESTATIONS

Dear children of men, as you may or may not know, the physical realms of Earth is controlled by the Higher variegated realms of the Spirit. And the Lord of the Universe and the Universes is the Consummate Supreme Controller of all the variegated realms including the world of man. Thus, the Lord is the Sole Ultimate Controller of all manifestations.

Remember King Nebuchadnezzar of the ancient Babylon; when he became recalcitrant and proud, claiming to be the controller of the situations in his kingdom, the Great Ones above, Watchers in the Heavenly realms of Light, descended on him. Then his heart was changed from that of man to that of beast, **"that the living may know that the Most High ruleth in the kingdom of men".** (See Dan. 4).

Now, in the Spirit I was caught up into the Supreme Chamber of the holy gods, presided over by God in His manifestation as the King of Kings and Lord of Lords. Here, decisions are made on diverse realms of existence.

Earthmen, remember it was said of old: **"Thou shalt not revile the gods"** (Exo. 22:28). The aforementioned holy gods here have nothing to do with the 'paramount gods' of the tribes, secret societies and nations of men that lead astray; that have no portion in the Heavenly realms of Light, of the Lord of Hosts. Rather, the holy gods are the Great Ones, the Sons of God, who appear in the realms beyond, in the Inner Chamber of the One Eternal King of Kings and Lord of Lords. They are in certain terms the Great Spirits of God in His Light, in all the Universes of God.

Also, remember the Scriptural evidence of **"When the sons of God came to present themselves before the LORD"** (Job 1:6; 2:1); when in the realms beyond **"The morning stars sang together, and all the sons of God shouted for joy"** (Job 38:7); as well as when mighty Spirits stood by the LORD and made suggestions wherein the case and fate of Ahab, king of ancient Israel, was decided. (See 1 Kings 22:19--22). These great Spirits, these Sons of God, are the holy gods.

DIVINE DECISIONS SET FORTH

In the Spirit I was caught up into the holy meeting chamber of God and the holy gods, and the Lord of Hosts sat upon His Throne. Now, regarding the year 2018 wherein this was revealed to the Harbinger of the Last Covenant, the first thing spoken from the Throne was: **"I have made this year to be very good to all My chosen ones on Earth".**

Earthmen, the hardship faced in the world of man, because of the wicked thoughts, words and actions of the children of men, who have no portion now in the divine inheritance of 'The Redeemer of the Oppressed' in Light, came before the Throne. A verdict was reached and passed. What appeared to me as a last warning was sent forth from the Throne to the Earth-world.

It was decreed from the Throne that those who block the ways of progress for others, many thereof, in different enclaves, organisations of men, families, communities, amongst others, will be removed from the face of the Earth, beginning from 2018 to the years ahead as never before. Mighty Angels were stationed in duty posts, and to them the implementation of this was assigned.

Those that sit on the fence, who refuse to enter into the Light of the Almighty, and who hinder others from entering, many thereof, were brought low. Even those that work for the increase of iniquity, the false prophets, the sorcerers and necromancers that lead astray, will have as their portion greater afflictions and will be more chastised from thence to the years ahead.

GREAT DIVINE ASSIGNMENT

The nation whose enclave is held bound by high manipulations of darkness, whose abode and seat of power is now the chamber of the most vicious astral forces, was found guilty of reviving the abolished craft. A craft abolished by the Ancient of Days Himself, which operational sustenance lies in the Fingers of the King of Kings and Lord of Lords.

Earthmen, in the years gone by,(but still in our time), the Ancient of Days manifested and stood upon the Asteroid Belt between the Planets Mars and Jupiter. This is the region which the mundane scientists of Earth initially considered the leftover materials in the composition of the Solar System, but which in reality is the debris of exploded Planet, caused by multiple atomic radiation. The Ancient of Days set this at naught for the world of man, by the Supreme standard of the Almighty, which is Himself.

This was done by the eternal decree of The Holiest of the Holy, which can't change. It was then decreed by **'The Landlord of the Universe'** that the Earth Planet will not be destroyed by atomic bomb and that the use of same anymore for war among men is put out of use.

The nations of men, be it America, Russia, Britain, France, North Korea, China and others are now incapacitated by the Lord of Hosts from waging atomic war on Earth. And for this purpose, the spirit of the leader of a nation embedded in this, and the vicious astral entities guiding the realm of his throne, were brought low before the Throne of the Lord of Hosts. They were disarmed whilst the astral ones in chains were taken to a realm of the dark enclave outside the Solar System.

By the decree of the Lord who sits on the Throne, certain Ancient Ones from the realm of **"the bright and morning star"** (Rev. 22:16), with extraordinary extraterrestrial equipment, far beyond what the human words can describe, radiated Divine Light round the Earth Planet seven times, according to the number of the Seven Spirits of God, in the great intervention of Divine assignment.

This strengthened the Earth-world for her to rise in the greater Light of God, but not with the sons of perdition. This magnified the potency of several billions of Divine-Coordinate-Points spread upon the surface of the Earth into a factor of above 500 times. Furthermore, this added Light to Light, for the victory of Light in the greatest war of Light and Darkness that must come upon the people of this world.

Earthman, anywhere you are upon the face of the Earth now, you are surely not far from a Divine-Coordinate-Point, each which is magnified from 2018 to the years ahead. And some of you are even dwelling, in human terms, upon the location of such points. Beware such ones; beware Oh children of men, for whatever is your mental pattern – thoughts, words and deeds – on such locations, will be magnified and returned to you as never before.

Again, by the radiation of Light round the Earth, Power was added to the three Ancient Ones themselves, who descended from above in our time. Residing in the innermost circle of the core of the Earth, they reside in a region of Earth which even some great Angels of Light can't access. These have come in our time to guard the realm of "the God of the Earth" (Rev. 11:4), solely for the ascent of the earthmen in Light.

NATIONS OF THIS WORLD

And it came to pass that I received His Words for some nations of men, beginning with Nigeria. Of Nigeria, He who sits on the Throne said to me:

"Harbinger of the Last Covenant, your land (Nigeria), brought together as one for a reason of good for your world not known yet to many, will surely not be divided. Behold, My decree of oneness upon all generations of your land stands steadfast before Me. The true balance of oneness, which for years have eluded the people of your land, will now be enacted not by the force of arms, not by the anger of those that are led, but the hour will come, according to the time of life, that I will bring this up with My Finger and bring it to pass in peace".

I learnt before the Throne, as was made known to me severally in the past, that the agitations for the division of Nigeria into smaller nations, have no place in the divine plan of the Almighty for Nigeria. Also, in the days ahead, the quest for domination of one over the other, will be subjugated. Then fair play, equity and justice for all will reign. Again, He said to me:

"Behold, I am in the midst of thee, even your land. My Spirit of Peace will have an increase in your land as never before, and of My Blessings thereof, none will take away. Behold, one with the heart of a dove for the good of the people of your land, is already in your midst; awaiting the call to move your land to the next stage with the oil of helpfulness.

"Behold, in his abode dwells the great Spirit of a race that is already awakened.

Coming forth from a rising Sun, Oh Harbinger of the Last Covenant, in a capacity beyond what he is, which this day is given that only himself will grant in Me; by submission, by supplication to the banishing of the iniquity of the land;

behold, by the spirit of agreement in the abode of a great queen, My chosen one; I have made him the star-point of reference for the rise of your land before Me".

Then, he was brought before the Throne. And to some, for; and to some, against. He was weighed and a percentage was increased. A clause was made, to negate reversal, that he should not sow in the flesh; and in humility, as was said, he must stand by the 'Moses' of his time.

In the Spirit, I saw a great curse hovering; a curse upon the nation Nigeria. Then I wept. The curse upon a great nation for the murder of her leaders, for the murder of millions of innocent souls, for joining iniquity to iniquity for the increase thereof, for the oppression of the poor, for the practice of falsehood in worship of the man-made-gods, and above all for blasphemy of The Holiest of the Holy. Corruption in almost all fabrics of the nation, became the instrument for which the curse gained the right of operation.

Can't you see this, children of the land? Where are you now? Where is the Nigerian Airways today? Nigeria, did you not help to feed Ethiopia in her past years of the predicament of draught? Today, her Airline is one of the pride of Africa while yours is gone. Stable light of electricity is not found in you, Oh Nigeria. Your leaders steal your wealth, infested with the spirit of the great curse, and stack them in other lands, whilst your land wallow in darkness.

Lesser lands than you, even your neighbours, Benin Republic and Togo, enjoy far more stable light than you, Nigeria. How can your industries flourish without light? In this present age, how can you grow as a nation without light? You are mocked as some of your children have become slaves in other lands. Some of your so-called 'high chiefs' are in reality 'high thieves' in your midst.

Remember, Oh Nigeria, that in the past you cast aspersions on Ghana. You sent her children away with a bag of mockery tagged 'Ghana must go'. But today, she is far ahead of you on the basis which bring forth the growth of a nation – electricity. Your children now go to her Universities on a better ground. In prudence ahead of you, she manage the little resources given to her.

Nigeria, were you not at the same level at your independent with Brazil, Singapore, Taiwan and even ahead of Malaysia? Today your children visit these lands as if they are 'going to heaven'. Are you not one of the major producers of crude oil on Earth? Yet you import fuel and from time to time your children have no easy access to it. What about your currency? Was it not equal to the British Pounds and above the American Dollar in the past? Where is the strength of your currency today? Can't you see the great curse at work? As I wept in the Spirit, for these amongst others, He who sits on the Throne spoke again and said:

> ***"Oh ye Harbinger of the Last Covenant, blessed be your land. By My Presence, the great curse upon your land will be broken; behold, now it is done. Behold, My mercy and victory belong to the camp wherein your tent is pitched.***
>
> ***Therefore, know and understand that this year (2018) I will swallow the curse and set at naught the right of discord. "Behold, the curse ignited by darkness for long against your land, I, even I, will surely take away. For the sake of My chosen ones, your land is now sanctified before Me. Behold, I will bring forth restoration and never shall the good set aside of old for your land be caused to flee".***

Then I leaped in great joy and paid my most respectful obeisance to the Lord and Master of the Universe, manifested in this realm of Light.

Furthermore, many other things were revealed to me in this holy realm. Now, it was revealed (2018) that:

1. The Spirit of the special 'Mercy of the Lord' will descend into Nigeria by 3.00 am of Thursday, 15th February, 2018, for a special mission unto the subjugation of the great curse, for a period of 20 hours.

Let those who have ears to hear be on fasting/prayer (6.00 am – 6.00 pm) that same day.

Take a flag of Nigeria, lift it up and make a prayer of Peace and Blessings for the land.

Endeavour to do so with a pure heart, without grudges against no one. Do this at any time within the aforementioned period.

(This was done in diverse places in Nigeria and in different parts of the world).

2. Submit to your leaders and pray always for them; do not judge and condemn them, do not bear false witness against them or against anyone, and do not speak of what you know not.

3. A great Soul came into Nigeria, with a mission to raise a standard against corruption. He was a chosen one who came from the primordial lineage of the blood of Abel, but his mission was hindered by those who offer stones instead of bread. Because it wasn't the time appointed, this great Soul from the city of Kano, departed, yet set an indelible standard for all generations of the rulers of men.

4. On former President of Nigeria, it was first said then that he should continue beyond 2015, because in him was found an excellent heart. Nevertheless, at the last hour, this was reversed when a Great One before the Throne made strong submission for a mission against the great curse to ignite, even the awareness thereof, and for some reasons which I am not granted to reveal.

5. And you may say: 'Does the Lord reverse Himself for any reason?' And to you I say, yes. Earthmen, remember the case of the Prophet Moses. Was it not said initially of him that he would lead his people to the promised land?

Along the way, for some reasons, the Lord reversed this and Moses did not enter the promised land. What about king Hezekiah of ancient Judah? He was "sick unto death" and to him the Lord via Prophet Isaiah said: "Set thine house in order; for thou shalt die, and not live". Nevertheless, for some reasons the Lord reversed Himself and later said to him:

"Behold, I will heal thee: on the third day thou shalt go up unto the house of the LORD. And I will add unto thy days fifteen years". (See II Kings chapter 20).

6. *Now, at the appointed time, one with a strong spirit to chastise corruption was brought upon the throne of Nigeria, with a specific mission which, before the Throne of the Lord of Hosts, is a prelude to the standard against the spirit of corruption. In this specific mission from the Throne, he needs the sincere support of all the people of the land. His absolute tenacity to this mission, without fear or favour, with a transparent heart, is all that is required. Therein lies the success or the failure of the mission given to him by the Lord.*

And by the subjugation of the great curse, those who will come after him will never return Nigeria to the former things. Now, bear in mind that only a Head of State can't eradicate corruption in a nation. And let the battle against corruption never be politicised; it is a monster that we must collectively battle, till its dominion is no more.

7. *Three great trees, giants in every sense of man's mundane existence, will fall off in the land of Nigeria . And for the kidnappers, the terrorists and armed robbers, the hired assassins and ritual killers, they are living on borrowed time. As they strive to rise, let's keep praying for the Lord to transform them for good.*

8. *A party that ruled the land was shown covered by a strange leaf. Her rise again will come only when the strange leaf is taken away, otherwise the* *throne of the land will elude her. When she comes up, she will bring forth a lesson for good.*

The ruling party should endeavour to learn from the mistakes of the defeated party that reigned before her, for the good of all.

9. Human political permutations will no longer determine what happens to the throne of the land, and the thrones thereof, for in it many will labour in vain.

Only the dictates of the Lord will dominate.

No human political party will salvage the land, only the Lord of the Universe will.

Regardless of your political party, tribe or religion, we are one nation. Let's all join hands to build the land for good.

10. Illesha in Nigeria should be put in serious prayers; a vicious visit upon her, for the revenge of blood, will take human lives. Sincerely pray for this to be averted.

11. The axis of Okene/ Lokoja, the axis of Benin/ Agbor/ Ubulukwu, the axis of Taraba, the axis of Zamfara, the axis of Port Harcourt/ Umuhia/ Okigwe/ Enugu, the axis of Lagos/Ogun/Ibadan, and the axis of the North East Nigeria, should be put in fervent prayers, to avert the waste of innocent blood. Ritual killers will be strengthened by the forces of darkness, but the Potency of the Lord is the greatest.

12. *A sitting Governor will loosefavour and vicious 'hunters' will come after his life. Another will be 'transferred' by poison. We need serious prayers to avert these.*

Jerusalem: In the Spirit, in the inner chamber of the holy gods and the God of gods, before the Throne of the Lord of Hosts, the cause for the case of Jerusalem was brought up. It is written in the Holy Scriptures:

"Produce your cause, saith the LORD;
bring forth your strong reasons, saith the King of Jacob. Let them bring them forth, and show us what shall happen; let them show the former things, what may be, that we may consider them, and know the latter end of them; or declare us things for to come" (Isa. 41:21,22).

It is revealed that the curse placed on Jerusalem by the Lord hasn't been reversed, because the people of Israel haven't met with the condition required for its reversal. It may be recalled that while He was on the physical realms of Earth, the Great Lord Jesus the Christ, cursed Jerusalem thus:

"Jerusalem, Jerusalem, thou that killest the prophets, and stonest them which are sent unto thee, how often would I have gathered thy children together, even as a hen gathereth her chickens under her wings, and ye would not! Behold, your

> **house is left unto you desolate. For I say unto you, ye shall not see me henceforth, till ye shall say, Blessed is he that cometh in the name of the Lord"** (Math. 23:37—39).

This is the cause of the problem of Jerusalem unto this day. And He who sits on the Throne said to me:

"Behold, Oh son of man, the standard of the new Jerusalem (Rev.3:12; and 21:2) is set to salvage your world. The faithful should hope only on this. The order of the old Jerusalem, and the struggle to possess it, is gone before Me" . And for other things said in this connection, I was commanded not to reveal.

Ghana: The nation of Ghana was blessed and will ever remain blessed, for to her it was said: "With open arms thou has received the Light of God". Let the people of Ghana rejoice and let the faithful in her strengthen the weak. Her children will reap the fruits of good labour. Ghana: it was said that your leader, a chosen one, stands for the progress of all, and is given to you for good. Employment opportunities will increase in you; corrupt ones among you will not escape. Those withholding and sitting on the promotion of others will be chastised, and many taken away. Pray against floods that will destroy lives and property.

Open Doors: In all the nations of this world, the door of the good things of life is opened for all the chosen ones on Earth, from 2018 to the years ahead. Many of them will see the Lord face to face. Desires will be fulfilled. Many despised ones among men will rise; many among men who oppressed others with wealth will be made poor. The dead will come to life in different parts of the Earth. The unmarried, men and women, will be blessed with husbands and wives. The impotent will be revitalised to bear children. Those having stillbirth will bear living souls. The Sun, the Moon and the Stars will be made one. Dry hands will be blessed with money. Women who are subjugated in their homes will have the cause for joy.

The Hunters: Nevertheless, the hunters will still be on the increase in the world of man, even the daughters of men, who add craft to craft, and who are old in the hunt for the precious life.

Kenya: To you it was said that "The bitter cry unto the Throne, by a great woman, has salvaged you from fire". But it was revealed that a catastrophe in your midst will trap many to death. This we must collectively pray against. Kenya, you are blessed because of the chosen ones in you.

Air Disasters And Fire: The most vicious astral forces will stage a great battle in the air. Having gathered enough astral potency for battle, arising from the subtle aspects of nuclear energy and collective vicious mental pattern of humans, in conjunction with their manipulations of some mineral deposits beneath the Earth, they will fight the children of men in many ways. These include, but not limited to, plane crashes, strange fire outbreaks in diverse places, strange winds and floods. Now, be on fasting/prayer whenever you are travelling by flight. This will defeat the aforementioned manipulations. One person who abides by this will salvage others on board in the name of the Lord.

United Kingdom: In the month of November this year (2018), between 17th and 23rd, the British land will suddenly receive mysteriously a boon from the Throne. This will salvage her children in the years ahead, in a coming great catastrophe.

Afghanistan: The spirit of genuine womanhood, freed from subjugation, sent forth a bitter cry unto the Throne. And it came to pass that 'The Redeemer of the Oppressed', after the revenge of blood, gave to her the answer of Peace.

Mongolia: An event stirred up in Mongolia, in the floating subtle city of Shambala, sent forth an energy of great Light before the Throne, for greater inventions to come in the world of man in the years ahead, through the black race, for the good of men.

India: The collapse of a temple of Vishnu in India will take the lives of many. The visit of a strange disease therein will cause the fall of men. Prayers should be offered to avert these. But India will record growth for the progress of life.

Vicious Occult Headquarters: To all vicious occult headquarters in the world of man, it was said from the Throne: "Behold, I have abolished the craft, the wickedness, the gatherings of the hypocrites; all that will seek help in thee shall inherit the winds".

The United States: The people of the pleasant land will be strengthened to continue to play their leading role in the affairs of men. In the hour of fulfilment, a mustard seed that became a tree will take away her dominion. An invention will come via the people of the pleasant land that will work on its own via the thoughts of controllers, when the dichotomy of religion and science is removed. Natural disasters will occur, and the murderers of sleep who seek the lives of men. We should pray against these.

Democratic Republic of Congo: Great Light is found in thee, but not on the throne. You hold yourself down with blood found where justice should reign. Another will rise in your midst, whose face will cause the light of glory to flourish in you.

Liberia: The spirit of a false prophet will rise in the land that laid waste, but now restored; it will attempt to deceive the heart of the Head of State. The leader should seek sanctification from the Lord, and he will lead Liberia to greater heights of honour.

Star Number Three: The great gods, mighty Angels of Light, great Sons of God in a Heavenly realm of Mars, masters and riders of The 3rd Star, will visit the Earth again this year, and every year to several years ahead, four times a year, from the 18th April to May 23rd. Adding Light to Light, good to good, in the Holy Name of the King of Kings and Lord of Lords, their visit is for the good of all men on Earth, especially to those who will show selfless love with a pure heart. Time and space won't permit me to give further details, but suffice me to say that you should endeavour to always walk on the path of good, so that good will follow you.

Blessings Shared: In the decision above, in the sacred council Chamber of God and gods, the Lord of Hosts decreed the continued sharing of all the good fruits of the Earth. All the good of the Earth is shared to the chosen ones in different parts of the world. Volumes of work will be required for the details of this. We are in a delicate period of "hand-over". The old husbandmen are now handing over to the new husbandmen.

RETURNED TO MY PHYSICAL ABODE

May the Spirit of the Lord guide you to know where you belong in the new scheme of things that will unfold in the world of man. For therein you must work; therein is your spirit embedded. If one works where he does not belong, the gain of the fruits of labour will elude him. The Lord who sits on the Throne began to generate Power and Blessings as never before for the present generation of men, to all His chosen ones on Earth, unto the years ahead. And *He said to me:*

> *"Harbinger of the Last Covenant, behold, all who will maintain a pure heart, will see My Blessings; they will see My Power, for I will answer them with Peace! Go and proclaim this in your world; let the chosen ones publicise this, for the increase of My Blessings on them. Let all the chosen ones begin by sowing the fruits of labour to the things of My glory on Earth, not to the flesh. And this will speak for them before Me, for the increase of the fruits of Earth".*

After all these, I was brought back to the world of my physical abode, then I prayed and praised the Lord my God. Certain things revealed and said in this holy realm of Light are not published here, as I was commanded. However, in keeping with the Divine directive of the Lord of Hosts, this revelation is published in different ways for the earthmen in the world of man. God bless the reader, God bless His chosen ones on Earth, God bless our world. Amen.

MESSAGE FROM THE THRONE OF LIGHT

Now, look at the earthman; show him the way of life – the higher path of Light – he turns around and enters the forest of death. Show him the path led by the Great Lord Jesus the Christ that lives; admonish him to refrain from killing and maiming fellow earthmen, the practice of falsehood and wickedness, the worship of strange gods made by men, amongst others, he snubs whilst abiding in the deep forest of ignorance; in the dwelling places of a gods clothed in rags, wherein all that holds him down is his ignorance, that is, himself.

Earthman, you do not ask questions before you eat the free food of others. Therefore, I say to you: The questions you ask after the food of another had fed your belly is in vain; for in that, you are led astray. And how can you escape, oh earthman? I admonish you to follow all men with a pure heart.

Endeavour to do this at all times, so that the falsehood which the wicked minded ones play on you, with the sole intention to put you into the pit, will become a pit but not for you. This will become a pit to the ones whose existence is embedded in falsehood and wickedness against the mission of your soul destiny in the Light of God.

And I stood before the Throne of the Lord of Light, in the early hours of a certain day. The Eternal Lord, who manifested, said several things concerning the faithful and the faithless. Amongst other things, He said to me:

"Harbinger of the Last Covenant, say to the children of men: You call upon Me, the Almighty, to salvage you; but the questions you must first answer are these: Are you blameless? Are you spotless?

"Harbinger of the Last Covenant, say to the children of men of your time: Behold, danger comes to you when thou have no Divine direction in Me; when you are not directed by Me, even by My Great Spirit, in all your affairs. I direct all the affairs of the faithful in Me;. I manage all the affairs of those under My Divine direction.

"I give direction to the lives of men.

This is known to the faithful in Me.

I am the Lord of all. Behold, I have set a standard, the boundary, the demarcation, which none will ever cross. From the right none will cross to the left, and from the left none will cross to the right. Behold, even the water that you drink and the air thereof, I bring forth My demarcation line between the faithful and the faithless. Therefore, what direction do you have without Me?

"What direction have you that seek the harm of another, in your thoughts, words and actions?

When you have no respect for the lives of men and you lead unto death;

by no means will you walk or lead in My Light. Judgement in your midst is found one against another.   Oh you that add wickedness to wickedness, behold, you are old in grudges; do you have a portion in Me?

"I say to you: You have no direction in My Light, when you are engrossed in the thought of yourself to be male or female; when you think and attach yourself to be of a tribe, race or religion. These shall pass away and you shall stand alone someday as yourself in yourself before Me.

You shall surely stand alone someday upon that which the saying of 'God forbid' does not take away.

"This is the hour which you should use to stand alone in My direction, but not alone, upon a better ground, when your time comes.

Behold, you shall have a feast of victory in the tabernacle of My Light. You, even you, shall have My inheritance restored in you.

Rejoice, Oh you that comes from the seed of the righteous, for now it is done. Be steadfast always in Me. Let not the good of your spirit of old be reversed by pollution, by the inheritance of the unjust and be given to another; let not the flesh of the wicked, the evil thereof, come to you.

"Oh you that is old in wickedness, prepare yourself in wickedness. Prepare yourself, you destroyers of the Earth. In My coming hour of winnowing, which must come, you shall surely be gathered, and, behold, your place shall be taken away. Prepare yourself, you that is strong in battle; you that kill and maim, in the lie that evil shall not come upon you.

Prepare yourself, for behold I, even I, am prepared against you.

"You have not harkened to My voice of Love and Peace. Unto this day, you have of old prospered in wickedness; you have armed yourself by the multitude of your wealth, you have rejoiced in this and brought low even My chosen ones; neither did you know the great day of My visitation. Therefore, because you have derided My Divine direction, and has added wickedness to wickedness in the prosperity of iniquity, behold, the reward of wickedness and iniquity will surely come upon you".

I BEAR WITNESS OF WHAT I KNOW

Earthmen, it is said that when a child is crying and pointing to a particular direction, if his father is not there, his mother is there. Remember, a tree that was once struck by lightning is never scared to see the sky darken with rain clouds. A word will always stay around as long as there is work for it to do.

Blessed is the one who goes hunting for rats but catches elephant. No sensible man will spit out the juicy morsel which good fortune had placed in his mouth. Earthman, the psychology of belief systems, the pivot point upon which religious thought thrives, may lead upward or downward in the journey of life.

When a belief system suits into the nature of reality, it becomes the impetus for the excellence of earthman in the consciousness of Divine Light. When it is embedded in falsehood, vain propaganda and acrimony, it becomes an impediment to true spiritual freedom and serves as the core element of subjugation to the mental pattern of a 'believer'. Every believer must ensure that the elements of his belief system is in tandem with the nature of reality. This is the path of excellence in Light; it is the path of truth and worship of the Almighty God. To achieve this, you must endeavour to personally ascertain the reality of what you are told. I tell you here in this treatise that the Lord is real, but you are the one alone who must ascertain the reality of the Lord in your consciousness.

Never base your belief system solely on the basis of what you are told. For if what you are told about someone is a lie for instance, and you accept same wholly, then your belief system on that will be established primarily on fallacy. The worst is when you take a step downward by becoming rigid and obstinate on the path of a false system of thought.

When any information is passed to you concerning a person, especially a derogatory one for instance, don't just accept it without making effort to ascertain its authenticity. It is easier to destroy than to build. Remember, the crucifixion of the Great Lord Jesus the Christ was the outcome of false allegations and campaign of calumny.

This vicious campaign made in those days, with the sole intention of discrediting the Personality of the Great Lord Jesus the Christ, was initiated and carried out by highly elevated religious leaders of His time. These religious officials were seen by the people as properly situated in the position to offer 'bread' to the children of men, but they offered stones instead of bread. Listen to what they proclaimed in those days concerning Christ, as recorded in the Holy Scriptures:

"And the scribes which came down from Jerusalem said, He hath Beelzebub, and by the prince of the devils casteth he out devils" (Mark 3:22).

"Then said the Jews unto him, now we know that thou hast a devil" (Jn. 8:52).

"But when the Pharisees heard it, they said, This fellow doth not cast out devils, but by Beelzebub the prince of the devils" (Math. 12:24).

This was the belief system held by the high religious officials of the Jews regarding the identity and mission of the Great Lord Jesus the Christ. This was the belief system which they inculcated into the consciousness of the earthmen then.

Those who followed this line of thought, did so not because of any practical evidence based on the true result of direct investigation, but because they were told so by the religious officials that they held in high spiritual esteem.

The religious officials themselves, who caused the campaign of calumny against the Lord to spread, did so not because they actually had practical and authentic evidence of the involvement of Jesus in the occult practices of Beelzebub, but because they were bamboozled and bereft of the true recognition of the validity and Divinity of 'The Son of Man'. Thus, their campaign of calumny was a disguised mental act to cover-up their ultimate core spiritual ignorance and prime religious inadequacies.

Having this in mind, it becomes imperative for the earthman to be sure of what his belief system holds at all times, concerning a person or group of persons, amongst others. I have often stated that there is a strong relationship between what you hear and what you think. Thus, mass acceptance of lies play a considerable role in the minds of the earthmen, in the formation of falsehood and wrong belief systems.

To rise above this hideous platform of wrong belief systems, begin by not submitting your mind and mental pattern to false stories without any investigation on your part. In this generation, let everyone strive to rise above the path of the Jewish religious officials of old.

Now, earthman, you are aware that if you receive information of what occurred in a certain place, your understanding of the information gotten can't be placed on the same platform with that of the person who directly experienced what happened. No matter how much confidence you may have on the information passed to you by another earthman, your perfect recognition of what you are told will still be less in approximation to the one who directly experienced what happened in practical terms. Now, in this material, I speak not merely on what I believe, but solely on what I know. I know that the Lord is real indeed.

ESTATE OF GOODNESS

Earthman, always know and remember that the Lord of the Universe is real, more real than the physical world that you know. He spoke in the past, He is still speaking now and will continue to speak in the endless years ahead. In the Spirit I stood before His Glorious Throne of Light; His Word came to me and He said:

> *"Harbinger of the Last Covenant, say to the children of men: Do good and good will follow you; refrain from the path of evil and wickedness, for evil begets evil and wickedness is rewarded with same. "Blessed is the one who has more good to speak for him before Me; for surely his way is made smooth in the journey of life.*

> *When your deeds of evil prevail and speak against you before Me, even before the Throne, you will surely be brought low as you travel and traverse My realms of existence; even if you are lifted high amongst the children of men, you will surely be brought low in the journey of life.*

> *"And, behold, the journey of life of Souls, ends not with the physical realms of Earth, the existence*

that you know. Therefore,

let your good be magnified in the days ahead. Let good override wickedness and evil.

Let it come forth upon you, for the increaseof the good fruits and the true blessings of life from Me.

"I say to the children of men: When trials come your way and you seek for Divine intervention; in any situation in which you seek even for the help of the Almighty; behold, your records before Me will be examined. Then will it be determined what will or will not happen to you.

"Therefore know, Oh children of men, that he who abides in the estate of goodness, of love and mercy towards others, whose life is devoid of perpetual falsehood and tricky heart, needs only but a prayer of thanksgiving to the Almighty. He needs no prayer nor petition to Me for silver and gold, for wife and husband, for houses, cars and riches; for, behold, what belongs to him from the Throne must surely come to him.

Those who have ears to hear, let them hear".

POWER ENCOUNTERS

Now, concerning what was brought to the 'Harbinger of the Last Covenant', from the Glorious Throne of Light, for the year 2019 to the years ahead, for the world of man, I was permitted to say not the details but a little.

Full details of same were for serious committed intercession of seven great messengers of Light on Earth, chosen by the Lord Himself and made known to the one speaking here. They stood for the faithful and the faithless on all that were revealed. Within three days after the revelation, the chosen seven, in different parts of the world, were reached by me, as specifically and divinely ordered by the Lord Himself.

Now, let the chosen ones of the LORD of Hosts rejoice; let all that walk on the path of Light lift up their hearts in great joy; for, behold, your triumph over all the devices of the wicked, in all aspects of your life, is sealed before the Throne of the Almighty. Let the heart that reads this claim the Victorious Spirit of the Almighty, for, surely, this is your hour of greater Divine excellence in Light.

Oh chosen one, be steadfast, for you will overcome all that seek to hold you down, and no wickedness will be lodged with you; affliction will not dwell in your bosom. Furthermore, I was permitted in the Divine spheres, before the Throne, to make the following known in the world of man:

1. The great custodians of darkness, in many lands of the Earth-world, were disarmed in the fourth month of the year 2019.

2. One hundred and twenty mighty gods of Light from above, great Angels of the Most High God, under the Divine authority of the God of gods, the King of Kings and Lord of Lords, are already welcomed and ushered in. Their works now unto the years ahead will be done in different nations, including Nigeria, United Kingdom, Ghana, Indonesia, Senegal, United States, Kenya, DRC, Japan, UAE, Syria, amongst others.

3. In Nigeria, they were commanded to reverse the assignment of the 'Beast' unto a great surprise.

4. The great thieves, struggling for what belongs not to them, upon the pillars of two poles, even a 'Beast' of darkness, even another , yet a 'Beast' from the pit of hell; it was decreed that the assignment of deceit and dishonor, behold, the standard for blood, will come to naught.

5. The camps of ruine will meet the ruins of the Greatest of the Great in battle, whose 'war' is made in righteousness. In the cycle of the configuration wherein peace is taken away, behold, Light came forth and triumphed over darkness.

6. Final Words were spoken from the Throne, but not in favour of a 'king' of the pleasant land. Adjustment both in 'ways and 'words' will cause the restoration of grace, otherwise a 'throne' will be lost in the hour of fulfilment.

7. In all the families of the Earth, those despised not for themselves, but for faithfulness to the Great Light of Heaven, will receive special visitation of the Spirit of the Almighty. Upon them shall be vomited the Mighty Spirit of increase; and the mouth that spoke ill will speak good.

8. The bell that rings for the magnification of Light, has come upon the potency of increase, beyond a third part of the world of man, with the odour of mercy for all the chosen ones of this generation.

9. Great Light from the Throne of the Almighty, absorbed by the resident Forces of Light in the Antarctic region for the good of earthmen, spreading greater radiation of Divine Light from the Supreme-Coordinate-Point of the 'rejected stone', will cause freedom from oppression and vicious astral attacks in the lives of all those who will seek the Power of God with a pure heart.

INOSCULATE HEAVENLY REALM

Now, in another occasion, in the Spirit, the Harbinger of the Last Covenant was led by a great One from above, a Heavenly Being of Light, into the inosculate subtle spheres of God's Light in our Solar System. This was via a flight of the holy gods – the 'Sons of God' – great Angelic Ones of the divine realms of the 'Morning Stars'. (See Job 38:7; Rev. 2:28; 22:16).

These Extraterrestrial Intelligences are the great Ones riding in battle under the Divine Authority of the King of Kings and Lord of Lords, and from whom the operational codes of the 'Armies of Heaven are established. (See Rev. 19:11-16). The Harbinger of the Last Covenant was led by one of these into the region of grandeur and helpfulness.

Behold, I stood in the subtle region of Light, which is the boundary between the middle Planetary Systems and the higher Planetary Systems (Heavens), wherein dwell some denizens of the Heavenly realms of Light. Earthmen, the middle Planetary Systems includes but not limited to the Earth-world.

The one saying these things was brought into a subtle region that exists within the electromagnetic ambers of ethereal intensities. Surely, this transcends the human recognition of space and time. Behold, the consciousness of this makes space and time feeble in approximation to higher realities in the Universes of God.

This wasn't my first guided visit by the holy Ones above into this region. And several things that I saw, these I have seen before. However, this time most of them came under the ambit of a different reality of divine lessons.

For instance, it was in this particular occasion that the Harbinger of the Last Covenant saw a field of golden grasses, wherein an earthman was with a daughter of man, in the symbolic manner of playing around her 'garden'. (The lessons of that moment, in that aspect, received directly from the Lord, are part of the contents of my book entitled HIDDEN TRUTH OF MAN AND WOMAN, which all should endeavour to read).

Now, earthmen, we must understand that the mysteries of man and woman are the sum-total of the mystery of the Earth-world. In such terms, whatever concerns man and woman affects the entire Earth-world. Again, we must understand that Souls in their original estates before physical birth, are neither males nor females; they are neither Blacks, Whites, Christians, Buddhists, Muslims, Hindus, amongst others.

Souls in their original estates are identities far beyond the aforementioned bodily identifications of gender, race and religion. The camouflage systems of these material realities, though vital to the human existence to some extent on the physical realms of Earth, are ultimately discarded within the order of inheritance of the higher Heavenly realms of Light. Thus, there are higher divine spheres of existence that see the children of men as one family of humanity, irrespective of apparent mundane dichotomies.

APPEARANCE OF THE LORD

Now, it came to pass in this region that the Great Lord of the Universe – King of Kings and Lord of Lords – appeared to me. The great Angelic One from above was there also. The Great Lord shewed me a mystery of the Heavens and Earth in symbolic terms. I have published part of this in the aforementioned book, namely, HIDDEN TRUTH OF MAN AND WOMAN. Apart from what I have already published, the Lord Himself also said to me:

"Harbinger of the Last Covenant, I have already brought you to the accurate knowledge of My eternal truth that, in the years ahead, within the reference point of earthly reality, the Earth-world won't remain the same. I am everywhere, even in your midst, doing all things, and managing all affairs.

"You have heard about 'the One conquering', whose mission is to conquer. Behold, the sound of two thunderstorms already heard, will be heard in the year 2020, from the control principality of the overall dominion, which fulfilment was the rise of the last head of the beast.

"Harbinger of the Last Covenant, I set this forth

beyond them, even the power of completeness of the sharing of blessings before Me; from five hundred and seventy- three chambers of divine protocols arising from Me; and of the control of economy, but not of the old. Behold, many will be scornful in laughter, to their own perils.

"Behold, the old will surely give way to the new. And for those riding upon the destinies of others, shinning thereof in the camouflage of pretences, the crafts of double faces,

I have abolished the craft. In the years ahead of you, Oh Harbinger of the Last Covenant, your world won't remain the same before Me.

"And for the confusions and ragging wars amongst the nations, behold, the war of all wars will certainly come to end all wars and confusions in the midst of the nations.

I will end the wars of the children of men with My war – the grandfather of all wars ever waged on Earth right from inception.

But know this, that there won't be even a gun shot in the war of your Lord; in the days which will surely come to pass.

"Harbinger of the Last Covenant, know and understand that before the end of the third day of the seventh month of the year 2075, according to the time of your world, behold, it will be known

to all that live upon the Earth-world that I am the True Man of War; for I am the Beginning and the End of wars.

"But this I say: Let the children of men expect this from Me, any moment from now, but surely before the standard of the hour already mentioned; even the time of your world established before Me. For, behold, the flesh of the captains and strong men; behold, the 'spirits of the dead', what goes forth for them and what they go forth for, will feed the vultures of darkness in destruction.

"When the last war is accomplished, your world will be returned to a new world of love and peace, the estate of My Light wherein it was before Me. I will surely return your world to the forgotten 'Garden of Eden ', and all that live upon the Earth-world will recognise My Presence as the King of Kings and Lord of Lords. The people of your world always say 'nothing will happen', but let all eyes watch and see what will happen.

"Expect this any moment from now, for your time is not My time, but the time spoken of, will never be exceeded. Thereafter, the world of man will shine forth in the brightness of the shinning stars before Me, unto the years ahead. Your world will then rise beyond certain limitations and join others, who have for long risen before Me in the gestalt of goodness. Those who have ears to hear, let them hear".

I SOUGHT UNDERSTANDING

Several other things were said by the Lord in this region of Light. The great Angelic One from above, who led the journey, finally guided the holy flight into other divine spheres. I sought divine understanding concerning the things said by the Lord. I also sought understanding concerning my country Nigeria, and it was said to me, amongst other things:

"Harbinger of the Last Covenant, know this that in your land, even in the days ahead, flying foes, foxes and strangers that cast aspersions will step upon the toes of sleeping giants. Reverberations will strengthen the bellies appointed to eat-off corruption.

"And when the fruits of liquid soars, by exigencies beyond your land, behold, larger portions of the waters will rejoice in the Fingers of the King of Kings. It will come to pass that greater Light will be added, and surely your land will excel in the goodness of the LORD God Almighty.

"Harbinger of the Last Covenant, admonish all in your world to be at peace with one another, for the Power of inner peace is supremely at work now

in your world; and the increase thereof will rise unto the day of fulfilment.

"The Power of the Almighty in your world is henceforth withdrawn into the central pool of the Power of God on Earth.

Therefore, without peace, those that call upon the Lord will not experience His Power.

Many will seek the Power of the Lord and will find nothing, because they do not live in peace; they do not have peace and they do not give peace to others. Many churches on Earth will fail here, for before the Throne, they are empty and exist as mere social clubs.

"Your world now has another name before the Lord. Behold, even the name of two camps, wherein there is joy; wherein there is sorrow.

And your land, chosen for a purpose that is not yet known, but will be known, will lead the way in the hour of fulfilment".

ANGELIC VISITATION

In another occasion of divine visitation, the great Angelic One from above came into the abode of the Harbinger of the Last Covenant. This was in the early hours of Thursday, 7th November, 2019. I sought understanding from him concerning what the Earth-world holds for the children of men in the year 2020 to the years ahead. Amongst other things, he said to me:

> *"Furious hatred knocks at the door, in diverse segments of your world, Oh Harbinger of the Last Covenant. In the year 2020, behold, blood will demand for blood.*
>
> *"From this time to the years ahead, the gods of many will meet their waterloo, in the hour wherein the signet of the One Eternal Almighty God will rise to weigh in the scale, the rudiments of polluted minds.*
>
> *"All those who take pleasure in the practice of abominations, the wickedness thereof, should be warned, because they will inherit the wind from what they relied upon.*

"Behold, you that speak lies against the Lord of the Universe, by making falsehood to appear as 'truth', be warned, for your reward of pain, beginning with the year 2020 unto the years ahead, is in the offing, and you will not escape.

"The guiding Cherubs of the Central Sun, beyond the Sun known to the children of men, will speed up the reward of evil upon humans, through the established channels. Behold, even the reward of good will accelerate beyond the threshold of recognition.

"Beginning from the year 2020 to the years ahead, mighty wind will blow across the nations of men. This will shake even the Heavenly powers. At last, this will cause many to bear witness of the Light of the God of gods.

"The chosen ones of the Lord on Earth, you have waited; behold, you have waited upon the mercy of the Almighty Father, who controls Light and darkness. You have waited and your feet is found to be established unto the tabernacle of the Kingdom of God, from the foundation of the world.

"Therefore, because you are found worthy before the Throne, behold, this is your hour of celebrations. You will celebrate, and celebrate, and celebrate in joy.

Before the Throne, the celebration of celebrations

is performed for you, by the Eternal One who holds the supreme destiny of conquering and to conquer. "By this, Oh Harbinger of the Last Covenant, anyone found worthy before the Throne of Light in the King of Kings and Lord of Lords, must have reasons for celebration upon celebration, in the year 2020 and beyond.

This standard is established by the LORD God Almighty".

At last, this holy One (Angelic Being) lead me into a certain Heavenly realm of Light, where great Angelic Beings of Light above celebrate the Holy Blood of the Great Lord Jesus the Christ shed upon the Cross, from Wednesday to Sunday every week, from the time that the Lord shed His Blood. I learnt great truths and mysteries about the Blood of the Great Lord Jesus the Christ. The holy One said to me:

"The Holy Power of the Almighty Lord, generated in such divine celebrations, empowers certain Forces of Light, especially the holy Angels of war, to fight for the chosen ones on Earth. Beginning from 2020 to the years ahead, this will come forth upon the ambit of tremendous increase".

I learnt that, just as the earthman abhors the environment where pigs feed on human excreta, so these holy Angels celebrating the Blood of the Lord, in the days of their celebration (Wednesday to Sunday) abhor the environment where sex is performed; where fornication or adultery is practiced. They don't operate in such environments, even if it is a sexual activity between husband and wife.

These Angels enter into their duty-posts of celebrating the Blood of the Great Lord Jesus the Christ every Wednesday to Sunday. During this period, they loathe all forms of sexual activity in the world of man. To them, it is like a pig enjoying human excreta, but abhorred to the children of men. However, I learnt that they are off their duty-posts every Monday and Tuesday of the week. They help the children of men to fight many battles of life, to the glory of God. And it came to pass that one of these said to me:

> **"Oh greatly beloved Harbinger of the Last Covenant, say to the people of your world: Behold, you have committed fornication and you have practiced adulteries. Let these belong to the days gone by. Rise above that by which you sold yourselves to the dry leaves of the desert. For therein you inherited nothing but affiliations.**
>
> **Henceforth, refrain from these; and we will come to you with the banner of goodness from the Light of God that fails not".**

OTHER DIVINE VISITATIONS OF THE GREAT LORD

Again, in another occasion, during my programme on 'Total Spiritual Freedom', held in Sapele, Nigeria, from the 12th to 15th December, 2019, the Lord manifested Himself physically to me. It was around 2am and He came forth seated upon my bed; I was greatly humbled by His presence in this manner. Also, there were divine visitations of the Lord to the Harbinger of the Last Covenant, while I was ministering in Accra, Ghana, from 13th to 19th of January, 2020.

Here, some of the things that Lord of the Universe, in the course of such great divine visitations, said to the Harbinger of the Last Covenant, via diverse aspects of His manifestations, are made known. These are published here for the guidance of the faithful and the faithless. The Great Lord spoke to me for different purposes, to different nations and for the entire world of man. Excerpts:

Indonesia: *"Because of the favour which you have obtained from Me – Master of Eternal Light – this day, by the spirit of the one that sits in your midst; even My chosen one who knows Me not; behold, I will cause you to escape a terrible wind.*

But I will surely judge the paramount dark gods, the wingless birds, in your midst".

Switzerland: *"By the crafts of deceitful heart, you sit upon the loots of high thieves for gain, and you impoverished even the ones already pushed to the wall. Behold, you encouraged high thieves in the world of man; and I have found their strength in you. Therefore, because I have found in your gates the spirit of stolen things, only by restitution shall you be free before Me, otherwise what is found in you will speak against you; and in the years ahead of you, your remembrance will be joggled, unless you change".*

Ghana: *"Oh Ghana, a people of prudence, behold, it will surely come to pass in you that a 'rejected stone' will rise and become a head in you, for the good of all.*

By the Mighty Spirit of My Righteousness shall this flourish. You are blessed, and blessed, and blessed. Because you have opened your arms to receive the Power of Heaven, I have commanded Heaven to receive you unto Me.

And for the wicked minded ones in your midst, the false prophets that lead astray; that add iniquity to iniquity and make merchandise of My holy things, I will chastise.

My chosen one sits upon your throne, and after

him, even in the years ahead of you, only My chosen ones will administer in you.

The grand roots of evil will not prosper in you; the fruits of righteousness will speak for you".

United States: *"A great tree with the observatory eyes that sees the world; behold, you have prospered in My Light; behold, you have prospered in the darkness of things. Great darkness is found in you, and great Light has come upon you. Behold, in darkness you lead astray.*

And when I set forth to cut down the tree, the roots thereof shall not be the same.

"Behold, in My Light you will reborn; and you will lead no more in the dark things of secret places. Behold, I will put off the darkness in you with the Light of the waters of life.

I am the True Leader of the human race. "

Behold, a seed planted in you, a tabernacle from another world of My Light, will host a captain of the ship in you. The visitor, with a delegation for good, will link the Heavens to Earth, and Earth to the Heavens.

"Behold, different parts of the world, in the benevolence of fourfold unto 481,800 hours, from the inception of the going forth of this word to the Harbinger of the Last Covenant, will magnify the

Light of the King of Kings. And for several years beyond the aforesaid hours, builders of golden blocks, upon the signposts of 'captain of delegates', by the order of his principal, even the 'Supreme Faithful Captain of Hosts of the Armies of Heaven' – the King of Kings and Lord of Lords – will cause advancements hitherto unknown to your world. Behold, these will be found in the forests of the rejected stone".

United Kingdom: *"Can one who practice not what he preaches bring forth another closer to My Light? Can a double faced one salvage another when he has not obtained My mercy? If not by My mercy, how can one escape the terrible wind? What about the thunderstorms? Can you escape from them when they come?*

"Behold, you have obtained mercy and favour from Me, for My Feet upon you; but the dominion of the seventh head, I have taken away and returned to Myself.

In the years ahead of you, through great trials, you will be purified in fire; you will subjugate the experiments of violence; the 'new world of Love' will have a say in you; and you will surely know Me as I should be known amongst men".

Kenya: *"The mountain of mercy from Me has come upon you. Pray unto Me that your root in the son of Isaac, son of Abraham, will be fully* *established. For your inheritance will rise in the greatness of the new world. Honour your mothers, Oh children of the 'Speaker' in My Lightfrom old; behold, the spirit of genuine womanhood speaks good for youbefore My Throne. I have blessed you".*

Russia: *"Do I forget even when a thing is forgotten to the children of men? When one doesn't know what dismembered his abode, will he build again? Will what dismembered before not dismember again? Will the one who waited for the moon not walk in darkness at the end. Use your tongue to count your teeth, and consider what is ahead of you. "You have sat for long on the fence.*
Have you entered? And what mission did you take upon yourself? Of honour or dishonour? And of hindrance to My chosen ones, this has come before Me. Of what profit is a labour for the wind? Of what profit is the gathering of armsand in the reliance on that which I will cut down? In the years ahead of you, behold, I will pass over you; and you will know God as God".

Cameroon: *"A sweet end is better than an anguish beginning. The waters in you shall have a sweet end; but, behold, a sweet beginning of a mantle shall have an anguish end in you. You will surely rise in the rudiments of the new world in My Peace. This I will do, because of My chosen ones in your midst".*

Australia: *"The work of pollution in the entire world of man is evacuated through your axis. You stand in a way for yourself, but you stand in another way for the entire Earth-world. The deep holes formed by what is above for good, hidden from the children of men, from your world to other hidden worlds of My Light, are found in you. You will be purified in fire again and again. But, behold, your last blessings, in the order of My new world, will surely come from Me".*

China: *"A race from the 'shinning Moon' unknown to your world, behold, you have come of age. Now the hour has come, and you will figure out theconfiguration where Light subjugates darkness, because of the presence of visitors unwanted by you. Goodness will yet again flourish in you, but in the years ahead of you, through great trials, again and again, you will return your glory unto Me".*

Israel: *"I will show you mercy in the years ahead of you, because you fulfilled your mission; and in anguish you reaped what you sowed. But My tabernacle, taken away from you, will not return to you as it was; it will surely not return, Oh children of Jacob".*

Nigeria: *"I have renamed you, and I will rename you again. Behold, after the hour of a great shock, which will surely come, the city of goodness will* *become your dwelling place. Even your signet shall be scarlet; behold, it shall be white; for the symbol thereof before Me is Love.*

These are My blessings upon you.

"Agitation for separation and of rebellion in you will have an end in Me. I have gathered you as one, and I will gather you again unto the oneness of good things. And as for hard times, this awaits the thieves of commonwealth in you.

Behold, I will use you to show signs and wonders on Earth, for the overall good of the children of men".

France: *"Bring forth your glory unto Me, even unto Me, the Lord of Hosts. Be among those whose glories are foundbefore Me. If you will not, behold, a daywill come in the years ahead of you that My Peace will not speak for you. And for what will come to pass in your midst, for withholding My glory, behold, the blame thereof will be cast upon you".*

South Africa: *"Behold, I stand in goodness of you. Haven't you stood in hindrance? I, even I, collapsed the wall erected in you against you.*

But My Fingers were hidden from you; not by another, but by your own eyes that see not. Behold, I will surely gather you and show My signs in you, that the remnants will glorify Me".

Saudi Arabia/Arab World: "Oh land of Arabia, you set a seal upon the path; Oh Saudi Arabia, you sealed the sum upon the pleasant inheritance of the ancient path of Abraham, yet you know not what becomes of thisin the hour of the end. Let the living have in their possessions the resemblance of you, for the generations to come.
Let them have this for what goes out for you and for what you go out for.

"Behold, I have performed My promise unto fulfilment in you; of the inheritance of wealth and of the inheritance of the peace of Abraham.

Behold, it will come to pass in you, in the years ahead of you, that questions will be asked concerning what you were, which they shall hear, but seeing they see not; and they shall have a glimpse by that which they have possessed".

India: *"Behold, I will bring forth your old men from their secret places inthe hour of fulfilment. I will surely bring them out from their hidden chambers wherein they see the children of men, but the children of men see them not; wherein I have taught them and they know Me in Light.*

"Behold, they will come forth and add light to Light, unto the embellishments to one fold under One Shepherd. I will bring to naught in you the ancient practice of abominations; behold, I will abolish in you the devices of powers of dark things,

and the remnants will be set upon the Light of My Kingdom".

Libya: *"What you hate, but what you sought after for others beside you, has come upon you. The overflow in you will have an end in Me – the Lord of all that is – and I will judge the instruments of the overflow. My Peace will bring this to pass.*

"Oh land of Libya, your mighty men were brought down, for I found in you that which belonged to Me, which you took unto yourself in the manner of Nebuchadnezzar. When I sent forth a section of the Heavenly Hosts to retrieve that which belonged to Me, even to One that can't be shared, behold, the actions of one led to the actions of many.

But I will heal your wounds and salvage the remnants at last".

Lumberia: *"Lumberia, Lumberia; a nation that was, and is not, yet is: behold, I will bring you forth, and you will become the shinning star of all nations. This I will surely do with My Mighty Hand. Behold, Oh Lumberia, the Another Divine visitation of the great Lord pride of nations, the abode of goodness and of the New Jerusalem, you are the hope of the rejected stone.*

"All the good things, for all the coming generations of the children of men, are kept in you from the foundation of the world. Behold, I will build

upon you My twelve immortal foundations, and you will be clothed in white raiment. The Sky City, the Dove City and the City of Love, all are joined together in you.

"The banner of My Peace will be lifted in you for all. As of My Righteousness, this will stand steadfast upon your immortal gates; for, behold, you are the promised New Jerusalem. And after the great upheaval, which must come upon the world of man, behold, Oh Lumberia, the workings of My Hands upon you will be seen by all".

The World of Man: "Oh you nations of the Earth-world, you have heard that the nations of those who will be saved, will rise and bring forth their glories into My Kingdom on Earth. (See Rev. 21:23,24).

I will surely destroy idols from the face of the Earth; those who worship the unwanted things, the unclean things of the hands and minds of men, should be prepared to inherit the winds of fire.

"I will visit the secret chambers of strong men, even the fortress of dark places; behold, many shall be taken away in chains.

Weep, Oh mighty men of the Earth-world; you that is mighty in iniquity, weep for yourself, you that is old in abominations, for you will be taken.

Behold, miscarriage is better than what will befall

you, because for long you have sojourned in the dark places of cruelty.

"I have manifested Myself in your midst, in the true perspective of My Being, but you have refused to change.

Behold, I do not go out in search of your trouble; but you have troubled Me for long.

And when you trouble Me, you dig your grave. Nations will be saved in you, and in you shall nations be destroyed.

"Who is the person or nation that can contend with Me? Will the strength of America count? What about Russia and others? These are less than toys before Me.

Don't be worried about the wicked ones in your midst, for their end has come and you will hear of them no more.

Wicked ones will rise to meet their doom.

As a stubborn fowl ends in the hot pot of soup, so shall the wicked minded ones in your midst end in just a day before Me.

"This is the time of God in you, and everything spoken of must be fulfilled.

I have given you a long rope all this while; accept this final notice and change, or be prepared to meet your waterloo. It is pathetic before Me that the nations of the Earth- world do not know that the Earth has her own Landlord and Owner. This they will surely know".

Religious Murderers: *"Oh you children of anarchy; you commit murder in the name of your religions; you maim innocent people and rape the daughters of men. Behold, innocent blood is found in you. I will surely cause blood to go for blood; and blood will speak against you. You battle for the first inheritance, but you battle of your own, not of Me.*

"You have lifted yourself high and filled your high places with the nature of darkness.

Behold, you have behaved like a fowl that is drunk; and you have frolicked in wickedness. For ages, you have murdered, maimed and raped for your religions, in the name of a 'God'. I, even I, in fulfillment of the Scriptures, was murdered in your midst by you – religious leaders of men – in the guise of defending the God of Moses.

"You claimed to stand for the God of Jesus Christ; you erected a throne in the Christendom, falsified My holy path and used same to murder my faithful servants. You waged wars and committed mass murder in the guise of fighting for My cause.

Hitherto, you haven't changed. You shout that

'the Lord is great' in the cause of your bondage and killings, you misguided ones claiming to fight in defence of the God of Muhammad. Harbinger of the Last Covenant, many who claim to fight in defence of Krishna and Brahma; even the so-called religious warriors, who claimed to defend the lineage of Kumaras, have blood in their hands.

"Oh religions of the Earth-world, you sit on the fence; you have refused to enter, and you hinder others from entering.

Therefore, I will send unto you a mad wolf.

The fowl that is drunk will meet a mad wolf at last in battle. Behold, the eyes of the fowl shall see no more".

The Earthmen: *"Harbinger of the Last Covenant, say to the children of men with wicked hearts: Behold, for ages I have followed you with love and mercy. I permitted you to control the affairs of the Earth-world.*

This I allowed for you to change and imbibe the spirit of righteousness in Light. But in this, you turned to think that I am such a One like unto you.

"In this you gave Me a name; you called Me a friend of sinful ones. Oh children of men, be it known to you that I have no part nor portion with your sinful ways.

Because you have refused to change, behold, your time has passed before Me; and you will not escape the looming doom, which your wicked hearts will draw upon you".

Churches/Christendom: *"Harbinger of the Last Covenant, look at the Christendom of your time. Behold, before Me, many churches of the Earth-world are in shambles. They haven't risen beyond what you know as 'social clubs' in your midst.*

"Henceforth, whoever that seeks Me in the midst of the perishing shambles, seek but in vain. Behold, if one does good before Me, but belongs to no earthly church, I will receive him and cause his good to follow him. If one does evil and belongs to no earthly church, his evil will begat evil and he will reap the reward of wickedness.

"If one who belongs to a church does good before Me, good will speak for him before My Throne. If one who belongs to a church does evil, the reward of wickedness will be found in his bosom. Whoever does good amongst the children of men, good will speak for him before Me; whoever does evil amongst the children of men, evil will follow after his path. Those who have ears to hear, let them hear".

The War of Wars: *"Harbinger of the Last Covenant, you have heard that I will bring a great war on Earth, to end all the wars of the children of* *men. Let the mighty men of war prepare for war. For, behold, I am about to bring war to end wars.*

"I will surely punish the wicked children of men, for their ways are not Mine.

And concerning My ways, wherein lies My Will, these I will cause to prevail in all the realms of Earth at last. The children of men are indebted to Me; they are indebted to the Holy Spirit, even unto My Spirit that works all things.

"This is not because in them is found robbery and all forms of wickedness, but because they have disobeyed Me.
Behold, in their disobedience to Me is found robbery and all sorts of wickedness.

Therefore, I have raised a standard of the war of wars to cleanse the Earth-world ".

A New World: *"Behold, I have no part with the quest for high positions, high offices, in the world of man. I have no part with any political party formed in the world of man. While seeking after these, while acquiring them, haven't you followed the path of the Beast, even the path of falsehood and sinfulness?*

"Therefore, My pleasure, Oh children of men, lies in My chosen ones in your midst.

These are they whose blood are traced, from the

foundation of the world, to the blood of Abel. They are the possessors of My inheritance in Light; behold, they shall form the new world of righteousness and peace.

"And if truly you believe in Me, do not murmur at all. Do not complain about any situation, for there in lies unbelieve in Me.

I am always with the faithful ones at all times. My Spirit has no portion in all those who believe not in Me. I am the True Owner and Landlord of all that is.

"Behold, I have reserved a place for the faithless in Me, beyond a pole of the Sun. I will cause them, by mass transfer, even by the regeneration of spirits, to evacuate the Earth-world. Behold, they shall have a new beginning in Me, in the failed class of life.

"And it will come to pass that, in the years wherein is situated their rise from the dead, the faithful ones now in your midst would have risen unto the domain and dominion of the holy gods. Then shall the faithful in Me, in a thousand years ahead of you, visiting the enclave of the faithlessto guide, will surely appear in the garb of the holy gods. Those who have ears to hear, let them hear".

CONCLUSION:

Now, it was revealed to me in the Spirit (which I published online via the Facebook Page of Prof Iyke Nathan Uzorma, under 'emergency prayers') that some high profile chambers of the vicious astral entities (forces of darkness), seeking for the blood of earthmen and leaders of men, have launched specific astro-metaphysical occult projectiles into the eco-systems of the Earth-world, to cause air disasters/plane crashes in larger scales, in the world of man. I posted this revelation on the internet, urging the faithful to rise in prayers unto the Lord of Hosts, for His Mercy to come forth and subjugate this.

Let the people of Nigeria not pass over this lightly.

Pray for the safety of all; pray for the safety of those who lead you. Let the people of the nations of men take this to heart and seek the Spirit of the Almighty God in Light, for great war is raging in the hidden dimensions of the world of man. Our victory comes only from the Throne of the Almighty Father of Creation. This is the hour for us to truly be our brother's keepers. Let the strong stand for the weak.

Now, it came to pass that the Lord said to me: "Harbinger of the Last Covenant, do you know yourself as you should, in the eternal reality of things?" Then I answered and said: "Oh my Lord, Controller of all that is, a creature knows only what he is granted to know by his Creator. But, certainly, I know that I know nothing before You – the True Knower of all things". And He said to me: "You have spoken well, for what you know not is more than what you know".

Again, He said to me: "Harbinger of the Last Covenant, do you know that you were with Me from the beginning, even unto the foundation of the world? Enquire about this from Me, and surely I will unveil unto you the mystery of mysteries". And I said: "Oh my Lord, Supreme Master of Righteousness, have You made me capable of this?"

And He said to me: "Harbinger of the Last Covenant, behold, the voice that cried in the wilderness, behold, your voice was there. And the voice that answered to the one that cried, even right from inception, behold, your voice was there". And I said: "Oh Lord of Lords, neither do I understand the meaning of this. Is this said unto me alone, unto the entire children of men, or unto what I know not?" Then He said to me: "Harbinger of the Last Covenant, behold, what I say to you, I say to all.

What one man is, another man is. The difference is in the realisation of the true nature of things before Me". And I bowed in praise for the Lord of all realities.

So many other things were said for the world of man and for diverse nations by the Lord Himself, which now constitute the basis of my prayers to the One Eternal Almighty God. I was empowered for a special divine ministration on the faithful, for the destruction of unpleasant situations around them. I have also published some of the foregoing revelations online, via the Facebook Page of Prof Iyke Nathan Uzorma. Also, we have different divine expositions on the Prof. Iyke Nathan Uzorma YouTube channel. Endeavour to be part of the channel.

Our world is upon the threshold of great winnowing. The old will give way to the new. The Lord showed me the symbol of the dominion of Christ. He directed me to unveil this in the world of man. He also directed me to reproduce the symbol and make same accessible to the faithful on Earth, in final preparations for the colossal battle about to manifest.

By the divine direction of the Lord Himself, the Harbinger of the Last Covenant is working on this now. When we are done, you will surely be notified via different platforms, which includes but not limited to the aforementioned YouTube channel. That will be all for now.

A word is enough for the wise. Those who have ears to hear, let them hear.

Let eternal Peace and Blessings of the Almighty God abide with the reader of this material, in the Name of Our Lord Jesus Christ. Amen.

Yours in God's Vineyard

THUS ENDS THE HARBINGER'S OPEN LETTER TO THE EARTHMEN ON THE MATTER OF DEVINE REVELATIONS. GOD BLESS THE READER.

OCCULT GRAND MASTER NOW IN CHRIST VOL. 1

"For there is nothing covered, that shall not be revealed,' neither hid, that shall not be known"
-Jesus Christ (Luke 12:2).

"The foremost conversion testimony, renowned as 'The Jewel Of Exposition Of Hidden Powers.' A book of all times on the Highest game of occult deceit. It has opened the eyes of many in different parts of the world. "

Prof. Stephen Pinder Ejeh
Dean, Faculty of Engineering, Ahmadu Bello University Zaria, Nigeria

OCCULT GRAND MASTER NOW IN CHRIST VOL. 2

OCCULT GRAND MASTER NOW IN CHRIST VOL. 2 is A Powerful Exposition For The Total Liberation Of Man. How the Semen is taken and used to Enslave the Finance, Marriage, Health and Favour of people in different ways through Occult Mirror; How Diverse Astral Waves of Darkness are conjured from the Psychic Spheres against people; The Vicious Network of the Powers of Darkness and their Human Agents; How the Ultimate Power of Christ liberates from bondage; the true essence of Spiritual Warfare, amongst others, are all contained here. the Author categorically Stated That: *"If you are on the path of ignorance, the scales will fall from your eyes as you read this book."* Read This Book, Therefore, And Be Strong On the path of the Lord.

SECRETS FROM HEAVEN

" ...In the night of the same day the Lord appeared to me and   stood in my prayer room. This divine visitation was physical, for the Lord sat down and commanded me to write at the same time all that He would say. Then Our Lord and Saviour Jesus Christ spoke to me and said .... "

- Prof. Iyke Nathan Uzorma

MY 300 MINUTES EXPERIENCE OF HEAVEN

What are the departed Saints of ages learning now in Heaven? Who are the Watchers in the Heavenly realms and what do they do? What are the 'Seven Duty Posts of Silence' in Heaven? How does 'The Book of Remembrance' in Heaven affect humans on Earth? How do the recently departed believers acclamatize in the realms beyond? What is the true meaning of the 'bossom of Abraham' outside the interpretations generally given? How does the co-operative nature of existence operate in the Heavenly realms? What are the mysteries of the Lord's Forms and Holy Names? What are the Primordial Elements of Universal Creativity? How did the Angels come into existence? What are the two things that God is eternally searching for? Answers to these and much more are provided in this book.

81

BEHOLD I GIVE UNTO YOU POWER

What Power Did Krishna, Kammeje, Muhammed El-Muntaza, Moses, Paul Twitchell, Elijah, Anandamurti, Obribon Okpo, And Others Use? What Power Did Jesus Christ Give When He Sid "BEHOLD I GIVE UNTO YOU POWER....." Find Out In This Book, A Great Exposition On The Reality of Psychic, Occult, Esoteric And Spiritual Powers, In The Light Of Invisible Warfare, To Show How You Can Possess The POWER Above Powers, With Practical Evidence And Testimonies Of Victory.

DEEPER REALITIES OF EXISTENCE VOL. 1

Deeper Realities of Existence, is a book that holds for mankind a message of profound truth and revelation of hidden mysteries. It is the panacea to all forms of physical, psychological and psychic terrorism, including vicious Astral attack. This book elucidates the basis of Planetary Winnowing in this Age, the core terrestrial and extraterrestrial danger of atomic radiation unknown to mundane scientists, Universal Signet of the Supreme Mastership of Christ, Immutable Laws of the Universe, the rise of a sane civilization of Universal Brotherhood on Earth, amongst others.

VERSES OF GLORIOUS MARRIAGE

In their battle against successful marriage on Earth, the network of darkness established specific chambers in the Astral realms. There are two thousand minor chambers, forty main chambers and four absolute chambers in the vicious Astral psychic spheres coordinating the battle against marriage on Earth. In human terms, they are "special forces" solely for this project. Their operational guide is: "LET THERE BE MILLIONS OF MARRIAGES AMONG THE CHILDREN OF MEN, BUT LET THERE BE NO PERFECT AGREEMENT IN LOVE". These special Astral Forces fighting against marriage, from their minor, main and absolute chambers, operate well equipped Astral Satellite Systems. These Satellites, produced from the subtle fabrics of the Esoteric Solar Elements, collect, gather and store into the absolute chambers diverse vicious thoughts of humans. From the central pool of the absolute chambers, these vicious thoughts are radiated back to the Earth using the Astral super-conscious waves. These Astral waves invade the human mind, solely to form dichotomy in marriage, for a husband and wife not to live in perfect agreement in love. Why are they thus engaged? And what do we do to overcome them? Find out in this **Verses of Glorious Marriage.**

VERSES OF WISDOM AND WATCHFULNESS

Wisdom is the core nectar of watchfulness in the life of man. In our world, several wise men have, at one time or the other, provided wise counsel to raise our minds to the efficacy of wisdom. And most times those who ignored this have found themselves where they least expected in the hands of their enemies. It is only a fool that says he has no enemy. In 'Verses of Wisdom and Watchfulness', Prof. Iyke Nathan Uzorma has simplified the understanding of how to know and be watchful of the enemy and wicked minded friend. If we study this book and follow its instructions, the light of wisdom will rise to dispel the devices of the dubious minded people in our midst -- father, mother, husband, wife, friend, neighbor, colleague, inlaw, outright enemy, etc.

83

THE SEVEN CYCLES OF SPIRITUAL ATTACK ON MONEY

The kingdoms of darkness are advancing by empowering their own with enormous resources. Their human channels spend a lot, even using human blood, to obtain wealth from them, by which such humans are enslaved. Should we not also advance in Light? We should not only advance but overtake them, using our resources to promote the work of Jehovah God and HIS Christ in the world of man.
This exposition is coming for the first time on Earth.

VERSES OF ETERNAL TRUTH

HIGHER REALITY OF EXISTENCE

This treatise, 'Verses of Eternal Truth' is a book of the mysteries of life. It is made to explain the unexplained. It is good to be a child, but it is not good to remain a child. Man has come of age and this is the hour for him to know more. The true nature of the Sole Ultimate Reality (God), the core identity of man as spirit, subjective **experiences, multitudinous** dimensions and manifestations of Christ, forms of existence in the hereafter and much more, all are encapsulated in mystery. This book is set forth as a clue about the mysteries surrounding the existence of man and beyond.

AND THE 7TH ANGEL SOUNDED

FULFILLMENT OF THE ANCIENT PROPHECIES

The Bible book of Revelation (11:15) says: "And the seventh Angel sounded; and there were great voices in Heaven, saying, the kingdoms of this world are become the kingdoms of our Lord, and of His Christ; and He shall reign forever and ever". Saint John also saw in his revelation "a woman sit upon a scarlet coloured beast, full of names of blasphemy, having seven heads and ten horns". In his time, the great Prophet Daniel had a strange vision about how "the four winds of the heaven strove upon the great sea and four great beasts came up from the sea, diverse one from another". What these stand for, as well as their literal fulfillment on the physical realms of Earth, is what this book is all about. Also, on the little horn that grew up in the midst of the ten horns, "before whom there were three of the first horns plucked up by the roots", the eyes on the horn, the mouth that spoke great things, as manifested and related to our time, amongst others, including the heads of the beast and the last thereof in this age and time and much more, read this book to know more.

HIDDEN TERRORIST

RISE AND OVERCOME THEM

The elements of witchcraft, using diverse rights of the vicious astral system, have ruined, maimed and destroyed many people on Earth. Witchcraft attacks are not things to be toyed with. There are different elements of witchcraft and how to overcome them exposed in this book. There are certain high spirits of darkness operating as the strongholds of witchcraft. These include (1) Double Slayers of Destiny, (2) Eaters of Life from the Beginning, (3) Mighty Ones of Great Illusions, (4) Dry Serpents that Hover, (5) Carriers of Heavy Load, (6) The Dogs that Bite, (7) Midnight is Fearful, (8) Suckers of Blood, (9) Blood that goes for Blood, (10) Withholders of the Good, amongst others. These and much more are exposed in this book as well as how to overcome them. This is a book for all who seek the victory of Light over darkness.

GREAT DIVINE IMPACT

This striking treatise, 'GREAT DIVINE IMPACT' is a book of guidance for victory in the battles of life. it will open your eyes to the reality about the three stages of expression of the **Initial Creative Power of the Almighty;** how the third stage is your ultimate positive tool in both the journey and battles on Earth. find out the *Eight Supreme Armours,* the *Seven Divine Principles* as well as the *Seven Basic Awareness* via which you will be placed beyond the reach of the cosmic network of the most vicious forces of darkness. discover the coordinating propensities of the malevolent and benevolent realms beyond. understand the massages from the Heavenly realms of Light in our time, what Christ is saying now to the faithful and the faithless, amongst other.

VICIOUS OCCULT POWERS EXPOSED

'VICIOUS OCCULT POWERS EXPOSED' is set apart for the Light of Christ to excel. Here you will find out how to be firm and overcome al the elements of darkness; how the author prevailed over the hosts of darkness after his conversion; diverse occult devices used to enslave people, including answers to vital questions and much more.

OTHER BOOKS
By
Iyke Nathan Uzorma

1. OCCULT GRAND MASTER NOW IN CHRIST VOL. 1.

2. OCCULT GRAND MASTER NOW IN CHRIST VOL. 2

3. OCCULT GRAND MASTER NOW IN CHRIST VOL. 3

4. VICIOUS OCCULT POWERS EXPOSED (Revised and Enlarged Edition of the book first published under the title 'Exposing The Rulers of Darkness Vol. 1')

5. HIERARCHY OF HIGHER MANIFESTATIONS (Revised and Enlarged Edition of the book first published under the title 'Exposing The Rulers of Darkness Vol 2')

6. THE PATH OF LIGHT VOL. 1 (Revised and Enlarged Edition of the book first published under the title 'The Path of Perfection Vol. 1)

7. THE PATH OF LIGHT VOL. 2

8. THE SPIRIT REALMS VOL. 1 . . . A glimpse into the realms of the Forces of Light and the forces of darkness beyond the world of man (Revised and Enlarged Edition)

9. THE SPIRIT REALMS VOL. 2 . . . A glimpse into the

realms of the Forces of Light and forces of darkness beyond the world of man.

37. THE OCCULTIC STRONGHOLDS IN NIGERIA AND THE REST OF THE WORLD

38. LYING SPIRITS OF THE OCCULT VOL. 1 (Revised and Enlarged Edition)

39. LYING SPIRITS OF THE OCCULT VOL. 2

40. THE GREATEST REVELATION OF OUR TIME VOL. 1 (Revised and Enlarged Edition)

41. THE GREATEST REVELATION OF OUR TIME VOL. 2

42. WORLDWIDE SPIRITUAL BATTLES IN NIGERIA . . . Before and Beyond Abacha 43. FORMER OCCULT GRAND MASTER

43. NOW IN CHRIST SPEAKS VOL. 1

44. FORMER OCCULT GRAND MASTER NOW IN CHRIST SPEAKS VOL. 2

45. CHRIST: THE GLORIOUS MASTER

46. MIND RUDIMENTS VOL. 1

47. MIND RUDIMENTS VOL. 2

48. DIVINE REVELATIONS

PLUS OTHER BOOKS, VIDEOS, AUDIOS, MAGAZINES AND BULLETINS

9 7 9 8 8 8 9 0 3 0 0 4 4 7